Can Your Teen Survive—and Thrive—Without a Smartphone?

By Melanie Hempe

OTHER BOOKS
BY MELANIE HEMPE

Will Your Gamer Survive College?

The ScreenStrong Solution

Can Your Teen Survive—and Thrive—Without a Smartphone?

© 2018 Melanie Hempe

All rights reserved. No part of this book may be reproduced, stored in a retrieval system, or transmitted in any form or by any means— electronic, mechanical, photocopy, recording, or otherwise— except for brief quotations for the purpose of review of comment, without the prior permission of the publisher.

www.ScreenStrong.com

Printed in the United States of America
ISBN 978-1-7325379-0-3

Author: Melanie Hempe
Copy Editor: Amy Eytchison
Book design: Diana Wade

Table of Contents

The Coveted Smartphone	1
A Life-Changing Lunch	3
The Benefits of Delaying the Smartphone	5
The Day My Daughter Got a Smartphone—at 18	9
Understanding the Science	11
FAQs About Teens and Smartphones	23
How Can You Help Your Teens Now?	33
What if My Teen Already Has a Smartphone?	39
Don't Just Survive: Thrive!	47
Endnotes	*55*
About the Author	*60*

1 The Coveted Smartphone

Is it really possible for a teen to grow up today without a smartphone?

I often hear this question asked in a doubtful, hopeless tone. The short answer to the question is "Yes! It really is possible for a teen to survive, and even thrive, without a smartphone." But when I give people that answer, it usually leads to many more questions. That's when I share my daughter's story.

Our daughter made it through her middle-school years with a basic phone—and made it through with flying colors! Her older brother had struggled with a video game addiction, so my husband and I thought twice before handing over a smartphone to our daughter during those impressionable years.

I knew that more time on her phone would mean less time for other activities: less time at the kitchen table talking with her family after dinner, less time jumping on the trampoline outside with her brothers, and less downtime for reading and being alone. I also knew that having a smartphone would mean a lot more of a few other things: more time to gossip, more time to view unhealthy web content, more time to feel rejected from being left out of social events she could see online, and more time to compare her body, hair, and clothes to those of other girls.

But I thought that as a sophomore in high school, she was finally ready. After all, her friends all had smartphones. And I believed that she needed to finally get on board with the social media world. With her 16th birthday approaching, it seemed the perfect time to give her the long-awaited and coveted smartphone.

2 A Life-Changing Lunch

Right before her birthday, I was having lunch with some friends who had daughters approximately the same age as mine. When I casually mentioned to them that I was planning on giving my daughter a smartphone as a birthday present, their response was instant and clear: **"Whatever you do, DO NOT get her a smartphone—you will lose her!"**

I was stunned as they began to share stories of their smartphone woes:

"My daughter has one and it has been, by far, the worst parenting decision we've ever made."

"All they do is take silly selfies and stay up all night texting each other and Snapchatting videos instead of doing their homework."

"They take pictures of their food, their pimples, their socks, the dog going to the bathroom, or any other embarrassing thing happening at home. Then they send them to each other on Snapchat, Instagram, and on group texts."

*"At 16, they are still obsessed with silly, stupid middle-school jokes and bathroom humor. They are actually regressing and not growing up. **Don't do it!**"*

As my friends shared their stories, I listened intently. **I had been a mom long enough to know that the best parenting advice often comes from other moms who've made their own mistakes and had to resolve them.** Empowered by the wisdom coming from my friends, I changed my mind and did not buy my daughter a smartphone for her 16th birthday. I bought her some cute new boots instead.

3 The Benefits of Delaying the Smartphone

For our family, the smartphone delay turned out to be an excellent choice with a multitude of benefits. Here is a quick list of the perks we discovered by delaying smartphone use and, thereby, social media access:

- My daughter never went to bed in tears because someone said something mean to her on social media. Not once.
- She never woke up checking her phone to see how many "likes" she got before she could get dressed and proceed with her day.
- She never went to a therapist for social media depression or anxiety—a common new reason for therapy among teenage girls.
- She was detached from social media drama, so when she walked in the door from school, she really came home. I heard all about the day's events first before social media made them public, and I was the first voice offering mom-wisdom and advice. Teens need to feel

unconditionally understood and loved. If they don't find this at our kitchen table, they will search for it outside our home.

- She sought me out when she had questions and ideas, instead of looking to hundreds of digital acquaintances, or even strangers, for advice. She talked to us about moral dilemmas and current events. Her beliefs were not shaped by the latest opinions shared on social media.
- She used her brain to think through problems, instead of asking her phone for answers to every question.
- She never bad mouthed us (her parents) on social media as, sadly, many teens now do.
- She didn't repost, share, or "like" the latest gossip from school.
- She was never distracted by her phone while doing homework.
- She had more *real* downtime. She joined an art club and got involved in gymnastics. She read good books, and she actually enjoyed being alone.
- She played with her little brothers *a lot*. She took them on bike rides and played games and goofed around with them. She never ignored them to look at her phone, and they never saw any inappropriate content on her screen.

When we went out to dinner, we never had to compete with her phone at the table. Instead the night was spent on priceless conversation as we shared our stories with each other. I knew one day she would be out of the nest, and we would long for these irreplaceable moments. We got to hear all about her dreams of becoming a college gymnast, her fears, her opinions on current events, and all the things that made her the unique person she is. And we loved to hear her laugh.

We played cards and board games. We worked on puzzles together and enjoyed family outings and movie nights. We told lots of silly jokes and stories that reinforced a strong family foundation. She learned to trust that we had her back. We invited her friends over often. We were not her friends, but rather her loving parents, her life coaches who wanted the best for her.

When our daughter signed her National Letter of Intent for a full, four-year athletic scholarship in gymnastics at a large university, we (her family) were the first to hear about it, not hundreds of her social media followers. We relished that moment together. And I often wonder what would have happened if there had been years of social media drama, questionable photos, and posts laced with bathroom humor for her coaches to review. Parents and teens forget that social media decisions can have lifelong consequences, as even some celebrities have learned. Indeed, some people don't get recruited, hired, or married because of their past social media mistakes.

4 The Day My Daughter Got a Smartphone—at 18

A few months before my daughter left for college, I gave her a used smartphone. As you can guess, it took her about *four minutes* to learn how to use the phone. Whew, it didn't take her six years! Because she was still not an adult (the brain doesn't fully mature until age 25), I followed her on social media for the first few months. I made suggestions, and she occasionally asked me questions about things she posted. I witnessed her caution and her budding wisdom. Her use of her phone at 18 was certainly much smarter than her use would have been at 13 or even 16. She also got off our phone plan and acquired her own phone account at 18, the age that phone companies allow teens to get phones on their own. Imagine what it would be like if we followed that age restriction rule: we'd eliminate most of the major problems with teenagers and smartphones.

Her phone is not her life. She has not wasted years aimlessly trying to find something that her screen will never provide. Her rich, full teenhood was lived in the real world and not online. Even though she's very social, she has learned that she doesn't have to follow the crowd and give into all the cultural pressures around her. She did fine—better than fine.

Our daughter will have the rest of her life to deal with the responsibilities and stress of having a smartphone 24/7. As her parents, we had her first 18 years of life to create a strong, family-centered foundation, and we know in our hearts that we gave it our best shot, with no regrets.

When my daughter was home for her first visit after starting college, we were preparing to go out to dinner. I saw her smartphone lying on the kitchen table. As we headed out the door, I asked her if she needed it. She said, "No, Mom, I don't need my phone at dinner. I will be with everyone and I can't wait to catch up!" Her two giggling brothers were hanging off her like monkeys as she walked out the back door.

My eyes filled with tears of gratitude as I turned to look for the car keys. I realized that we gained much more than we lost with that one simple decision to delay her access to a smartphone. It really did change her life—both in ways we can measure and in ways we are still discovering.

5. Understanding the Science

Still not sure what to do? Not sure if your child can wait until late adolescence to get his/her* first smartphone? Here are additional reasons supported by science and current research to delay the smartphone for your teen:

1. **Building a personal brand causes stress and anxiety.** The 24/7 challenge of life on social media—constantly comparing themselves, being judged daily and publicly by peers, being bullied, and feeling pressure to conform—is highly stressful for teens. A 2017 survey of 1.1 million teens showed that adolescents who spent more time on social media and less time on non-screen activities and interpersonal social activities have more psychological problems.[1]

Throughout this book, "he" and "she" are used interchangeably to refer to a child or teen.

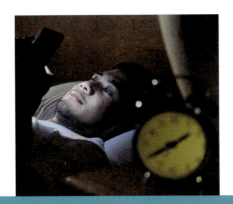

"The short-term, dopamine-driven feedback loops that we have created are destroying how society works."
—Chamath Palihapitiya, former vice president of user growth at Facebook, in "Dopamine, Smartphones & You: A battle for your time," Harvard University's Science in the News.[10]

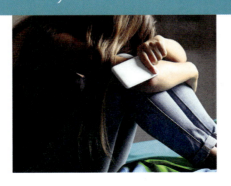

Growing up with a continuous overflow of social media, teens today are part of the "most anxious" generation.[2] More intense than stress, anxiety occurs when a teen fears not being adequate, not fitting in, or not measuring up to peer expectations. (While these are normal teen fears, they are amplified by social media.) Teens do not have the emotional tools, experience, or maturity to handle the constant demands of personal-brand (identity) building and the negative content of social media. This continual nervous and uneasy feeling takes a toll on their mental and physical health.[3]

2. **Higher risk for depression and suicide.** Chronic stress and anxiety from continual social media pressure can lead to depression. Studies show that people who spend large amounts of time scrolling through social media are more likely to suffer from depression.[4] In fact, depression symptoms in teenage girls increased 50 percent from 2012 to 2015, with a 21 percent increase for boys. The risk factors for suicide have also increased with teen social media use. Since the year 2000, teen suicides are up almost 30 percent. The group who spent the most time glued to their phones was 70 percent more likely to have suicidal thoughts.[5] Even perfectly balanced teens get off balance when they share their

problems in the world of social media. Relying heavily on teens to teach other teens about handling life's problems is an awful idea.

3. **Lack of sleep.** The health benefits associated with adequate sleep are many, especially for teens. Unfortunately, most of them are not getting their required nine hours per night.[6] Their phones are keeping them up, creating an overproduction of cortisol, the stress hormone. Elevated cortisol levels cause health problems for teens, including a lower immune response and a decrease in serotonin. Lack of sleep also contributes to poor grades, poor judgment, and poor athletic performance. Since teens are not always able to pinpoint which activities are making them stressed, like lack of sleep, they need adults to help regulate their choices and guide them.

4. **Reduced cognitive capacity.** Smartphone use is associated with greater distractions and less accurate responses to higher-level cognitive tasks. Studies demonstrate that the brain's ability to hold and process data is reduced when a smartphone is present, even if it is turned off. If the smartphone is on, cognitive capacity decreases even further.[7] It is truly a brain drain.

5. **Weakened parental and family attachment.** Attachment, or togetherness, is a child's strongest human need and most powerful drive. In their book, *Hold on to Your Kids: Why Parents Need To Matter More Than Peers*, Gordon Neufeld, PhD, and Gabor Maté, MD, explain that only a child's parents, not his peers, can meet this

need for attachment. Neufeld states, "Fitting in with the immature expectation of the peer group is not how the young grow to be independent, self-respecting adults. By weakening the natural lines of attachment and responsibility, peer orientation undermines healthy development...Peer oriented kids fail to grow up."[8]

Child and adolescent psychologist Dr. Richard Freed, PhD, author of *Wired Child*, speaks to this problem. Preteens and teens who shift their attachment from their parents to their devices and peers are at risk. Many parents mistakenly believe that this shift is healthy, but the more hours your teens spend with a phone, the more lonely and the less attached they will be to their family. Sibling relationships are also damaged by this shift.[9]

This point was brought home when our family was eating out one evening: I overheard a little girl calling out to her older sister, who had her nose in her phone, "Ever since you got that phone you act like you are not in our family anymore!"

Strong parental attachment serves as a buffer between children and the culture and helps prevent screen addiction. Neufeld concludes, "The season for digital connection arrives when a child is sufficiently developed and mature to preserve her or his own personhood. We must give them a chance to mature so that they can become the masters of these new tools, not their slaves."

6. **Setting the stage for addictions.** The use of smartphones is not a neutral activity. They are designed to stimulate a chemical response in the brain, delivering dopamine every time the user responds to a notification. Like slot machines, smartphones provide novelty and excitement, and both are scientifically designed to be addictive.[10] The bad news is that teens are at a higher risk for addiction because they become addicted more easily than adults. New discoveries show that when teens become addicted to anything, it changes the way their brains regulate the release of dopamine and their emotions—on a cellular level.[11] In her book, *The Teenage Brain: A Neuroscientist's Survival Guide to Raising Adolescents and Young Adults*, neurologist Frances Jensen says that the release of dopamine is enhanced in teens' brains, giving them a higher sense of reward than adults. Because the frontal cortex is still under construction and neurons are firing at a higher rate than those of adults, teens take more risks, and thus become addicted faster.[12] Their brains become hardwired to the craving, which

is why early addictions and habits are much harder to break. For this reason, 90 percent of all adult addictions begin in the teen years.[13] Setting teens up for screen addiction is more serious than you may realize.

7. **Decreased downtime.** Unplugged downtime, which allows time to process and think deeply about hard issues (without being tempted to immediately turn to YouTube or Snapchat), is necessary for creativity and innovation to occur. The added bonus is the reduction of teen stress and the rare feeling of purpose when you come up with an original thought without the help of the internet or 400 fake friends.

    An enticing smartphone can easily fill all the downtime in a teen's day. Just as snacking can sabotage a diet, little interruptions all through your teen's day can sabotage a digital diet. During these seemingly harmless pockets of time, habits are set and the battle is lost.[14] Ten minutes of discovering juicy gossip on Instagram on the way to school can sabotage her morning of classes. Ten minutes on the way home from school watching funny videos can zap that important conversation with you about a lunchroom conflict. Curling up with her phone on the couch during your family movie night reduces needed family attachment. The distraction of the phone during these transitions and pockets of time hurts teens most. It sets the stage for a lifelong dependence on technology to fill downtime; it robs teens of the gift of being present with people.

8. **Stunted communication skills and lack of empathy.** Healthy conversation and empathy are valuable life skills that are important for teens' emotional development and future success. But studies show that our teens are losing their ability to read emotions.[15] Hiding behind a smartphone can keep your teens from doing the hard work of awkward human interactions: maintaining eye contact, understanding tone, facial cues, and body language, and dealing with the natural pauses that are part of conversation. Practicing in-person conversations also helps teens tune in to the feelings of others. In her book *Reclaiming Conversation*, Sherry Turkle states that face-to-face conversation is the most human thing we do: "Fully present to one another, we learn to listen, It's where we develop the capacity for empathy."[16] *Caring* means that you physically go help your friends *in person* when they are hurting, not merely send them a text message or emoji. This connection might even mean sitting with them while they are crying or upset. The all-about-me nature of the teen smartphone world keeps the focus on

their own self-importance, reducing their social competencies and lowering their empathy.[17] Learning to care and to understand the needs of others will change your child. It could change the world.

9. **Diminished self-respect and self-control.** When teens share too much on social media, the results can be devastating—even permanently scarring. Because of their underdeveloped frontal cortex, teens have a more difficult time holding back when it comes to exposing personal information. They tend to post every thought that pops into their heads, even if it might be hurtful. Constantly sharing videos, images, and memes creates a feedback loop that can perpetuate poor decision making. In an environment where teens spend nine hours a day using some form of online media, they can be heavily influenced by this "all-about-likes" culture that can lead to disappointing, life-altering decisions.

10. **Unnecessary temptations.** Kids with smartphones typically view more porn than kids without them. The secret nature of a smartphone makes it easier to view and access pornography. Teen brains crave novelty and forbidden content. Porn exposure correlates with depression, anxiety,

stress, and social problems.[18] Teens also have to use more brain power than adults to resist temptations. It is hard enough to manage a web browser's access on a laptop, so why should we put the temptation in their pocket? Furthermore, parents, not immature social media followers, should speak to their kids first about moral issues, drugs, drinking, and how far is too far with a boyfriend or girlfriend.

11. **Compromised physical safety when driving.** Twenty-one percent of teen drivers involved in fatal accidents are distracted by their cell phones. Eleven teens die every day in accidents caused by texting while driving. In fact, teen drivers are four times more likely than adults to get into car crashes or near crashes when talking on the phone or texting.[19] The earlier a teen develops the habit of using a smartphone, the more difficult it will be to resist the temptation to use it when driving. This major challenge requires accountability and strict limits set by parents for their teens.

6 FAQs About Teens and Smartphones

Each time I share this story, the same questions come up.

Did you worry that your daughter wouldn't understand your decision or be mad at you?

No. We learned through raising our oldest son that fear of your children being angry is never a sound basis for any parenting decision. Over time, our confidence grew and so did hers; she trusted us, and I knew she would understand the importance of our decision one day. We took the power and control away from the phone with our decision, and it was pretty liberating. I did not care about being the cool mom or having cool kids. I also realized that if she was going to be mad at me forever over not giving in on the smartphone/social media decision, we had much bigger problems to address. Finally, I knew that it was unwise to let a teen have a vote on really big decisions. And giving your child daily access to a smartphone is a really big decision. They may be intellectually smart, but they are not yet wise. They do not have years of experience like parents do. We needed to take a step back and trust the brain science and our own parental wisdom.

> *"We do not want our children to be followers of the crowd. We want them to be leaders. When we allow our children to have something that we know they are not mature enough to handle, for the sake of fitting in, we are teaching our children to follow the crowd. It is our job to do what is right for our children, not to allow outside influences to decide that for us."*
> —*Thomas Kersting*, Disconnected: How To Reconnect Our Digitally Distracted Kids

Did you feel like you were overprotecting her?

Overprotecting, no. Protecting, yes. My daughter was learning to be independent, making decisions on her own. A smartphone is actually like a "blankie" as it can keep teens stuck in an unhealthy, immature stage. They hide behind their phones, using them to make mean comments and to avoid the natural, healthy conflicts that are part of face-to-face peer relationships. Building an adult is a process that takes time and patience. If the stages are rushed or skipped, disaster often follows. It is our job to guide teens during these critical years and train them to be independent in the real world first, not dependent on a virtual one.

Did your daughter feel that she was left out?

No. She had an active social life. If she was left out, she never knew it. Her peers on social media felt much more left out than she ever did. She

didn't have the large number of virtual friends in high school like most of her classmates, but she said she had deep friendships, which many young people today lack. She had texting on her basic phone, so she was able to reach different friend groups. She also says that many of her friends came to her for advice on social media drama because they knew she was a truly unbiased third party. The only time she felt left out was when her friends would come over and spend their time looking and laughing at their phones when she was sitting right there in front of them.

Did she "binge" and "go crazy" when she finally got her smartphone?

No. I know many parents worry about this. In fact, this is a major concern parents seem to have when struggling with the decision. When she did get her phone, she was older, more mature, and had established good habits such as time management and social skills. When she got to college, she didn't go crazy with social media. She continued to pursue all the other activities that fulfilled her, and her phone became the tool it was meant to be. Because social media overuse wasn't an ingrained childhood habit (the hardest to break), she knew when to cut back on phone time if it caused her too much stress. She had knowledge and confidence in her ability to do this. She even turned the phone off at night so it wouldn't wake her up. Moreover, she didn't use it when she was driving.

Why didn't you try a teen smartphone contract?

I observed and took the advice of every parent I know who told me phone contracts don't work. Teens do not take phone contracts (or any contract, for that matter) seriously, and, when it comes to their phones, they often lie. The very idea that the phone decision needed a contract was also a red flag. Parents are like coaches and coaches have rules, not contracts, with their non-adult players.[20]

Were you concerned that your daughter was not going to be prepared for the digital world?

Not at all. She's a bright girl. Social media is just another form of entertainment. It is not building rare or valuable skills for our kids' futures, and it is certainly not worth taking time away from other important skills they need to learn. Social media is simply designed to grab their attention. It collects their personal information, their likes and desires, and mashes them all together in an algorithm that can be used for marketing products and services to them. Is it all bad? No. But it is an extremely addictive, distracting, and potentially harmful form of entertainment. Since teens are excellent with the accelerator and lousy with the brakes, most are unable to use social media in moderation.

As a nurse, I already knew that teens have a hard time controlling their impulses and calculating risks due to their underdeveloped frontal cortex. They naturally gravitate toward low-effort/high-reward activities. Teen girls, especially, struggle with self-esteem issues. I also knew that smartphones tempt and encourage young people to share too much information. They tend to grow more reckless the more they use social media. Some teens I know have made lack of privacy mistakes that turned out to be life-altering. Adults keep hoping that if we put them on

social media long enough while trying to train them to use it well, our tweens and teens will mature faster. But we can't speed up this process; discretion only grows over time. Once teens become proficient in using self-control in real life, only then will that self-control transfer to their screen life. My daughter is much more prepared for the digital world as a result of practicing real life skills, not as a result of collecting a record-breaking number of "likes."

Was she bored every day without a smartphone?

No. Children who constantly check their phones are apt to be more bored than those who don't. They become helpless when they try to think of things to do offline in the real world. As they let the screen entertain them, they lose their ability to innovate and imagine. My daughter never complained about being bored. Instead she found many other things to do, including reading, art, and social activities with her team. Even today she still pulls out her art supplies when she has downtime because that is what she did to fill downtime during her high school years.

Did you worry that she would be behind when it came to using technology in her future job?

No. Teens don't learn useful technology skills on social media platforms. They don't learn nonverbal communication skills, empathy, respect, or writing skills on their phones, either. When she is interviewing for her first job, she will need the following abilities: using a firm handshake, speaking in proper and complete sentences, asking questions of the other person and waiting patiently for answers, maintaining eye contact, standing up straight, and responding to social cues. Business owners know that these skills are rare and more valuable than tech skills, which can be easily taught. Young people with good work habits and strong face-to-face communication skills will be way ahead in the job market of the future. Perhaps this is one reason why so many technology executives delay smartphone use for their own children.[21]

Did she regret not having a smartphone or social media?

No. When asked by a group of moms if she hated her parents for not allowing her to have a smartphone, my daughter confidently told them that she loved her family. She explained that while she did not have tons of social media followers in high school, the relationships she built were developed over time and *in person*. As a result, she learned how to be a true, loyal friend and how to seek out those same qualities in others. She has no regrets.

7 How Can You Help Your Teens Now?

Take the necessary steps to help your teens balance screen time, whether they have their own smartphone or not. They need your guidance to build good habits.

1. **Help them develop life skills.** It is easy to forget the importance of practicing life skills when technology gets in the way. Your kids will actually let you know when they are ready for a basic phone or a smartphone. If they don't know how to clean their room, organize their personal belongings, clean the bathroom (the way you do), do their own laundry, or cook a full meal, they are not ready for a phone.

2. **Limit the time they spend on their devices if they have them.** Teens are generally not good at setting limits on anything. They need

your help. Give them limits and stick to your guns: no smartphones after 10 p.m., no phones during homework, and limit social media checks to 20 minutes, if at all. Have a shared family social media account on your phone if you feel it is necessary, and delay individual smartphones until

your teen has developed the life skills needed to handle it properly. The teen years fly by so fast. They will have the rest of their lives to be on screens. Give them this gift for a few years.

3. **Increase in-person social interactions with their friend groups.** Offer to have their friends over often. Cook for them or have them cook (dinner/movie theme nights are fun). Get a portable fire pit for the backyard or arrange a board game night. Think of anything you can do to promote non-tech social time with their friends. It doesn't have to be complicated, but they will likely need your help to do this.

4. **Help them find new non-tech hobbies and extracurricular interests.** Expand your teens' world by exposing them to new hobbies. Help them seek out peers with interesting hobbies. Studies show that teens do much better when they are engaged in two extracurricular activities during high school.[22] This will get them out of isolation and into a social setting. It will also help them gain new interests and skills, which will lead to more purpose, meaning, and confidence.

5. **Know exactly what they are doing on their screens for homework and entertainment.** Screen privacy from parents is not a healthy choice during teen years. Having your child do homework in an open and accessible part of the home (kitchen or dining room table) helps reduce distractions and inappropriate screen use. Watch movies and sports together as a family; no more private screen entertainment.

6. **Go the extra mile to draw them into your family even when you are tired and they are moody.** Do not get down in the dumps with them. Instead smile a lot and use humor to break through the emotional tension. Remember, their reasoning center is not maturing as quickly as the emotion center in their brain. They need you to offer the emotional balance they don't have quite yet. Continue to interact and have conversations every day to strengthen family attachment.

7. **Make exercise a priority in your family.** Encourage your kids to enjoy sports, biking, hiking, and anything outdoors. Schedule active time each day. Turn your family time into time in nature.

8. **Help them get more sleep.** Teens need nine hours of sleep each night. Buy an alarm clock and don't allow phones or phone chargers in the bedroom.

9. **Get them involved in meal planning and cooking.** Let them help create a nutritious meal plan and cook the dishes alongside you. The meal delivery kits are a perfect, fun way for your kids to learn to cook. Have them create their own recipe book now to log their culinary accomplishments. Nothing beats a teen who knows how to cook!

10. **Spend more time with your teens.** Be interested in their lives and ask a lot of questions (without being annoying). Ask more about their friends and how they are doing and less about their grades. Affirm and appreciate them for their unique gifts and personality. Listen more than lecture and discover special, simple routines to do together. Choose to make time for purposeful conversations, but also remember that just being together in silence is powerful, too (fishing, biking, reading together). Don't forget that those little hugs and family traditions go a long way. The family stories that inevitably result from spending time together will last a lifetime.

8 What if My Teen Already Has a Smartphone?

You love your child. You did your research. And at the time, you made the wisest decision that you could about the best age for a phone. Now your teen has a smartphone, but you're having second thoughts. You see some benefits of the phone—convenience, for starters. But more than likely you also see more problems with distraction than you expected when the phone experiment began in your home. One thing is certain—your teen spends too much time on the phone. She may even exceed the average nine hours per day in constant connection, managing her online relationships.

While the information in this book may seem new, you have long sensed that this screen distraction is pulling your teen further and further away from your family. You long for the days when your teen could come home, escape from peer pressure, rest, and be herself. Peer contact is healthy, but the 24-hour dominant, inescapable influence of peers is not. You now realize that when you handed over the smartphone, you gave your child a one-way ticket to hang out with her friends full-time. You essentially agreed to co-parent with the device. You are now in constant competition with the social media culture as your child is torn between parents and peers. But there is hope.

You have a few options. You can begin the process of limiting time spent on the phone (because teens can't) or you can take a break altogether to reset habits and give everyone a needed rest.

For some, taking a season off or downgrading to a basic phone will be

> *"Parents are all too worried that their children will be misfits if they are not plugged in. We should be far more concerned with helping our children realize their potential as human beings. The blindness around this digital technology is much like a blindness around the phenomena of peer orientation. What is normal is judged by what is typical, not by what is natural or what is healthy. This blindness has been exacerbated by our love affair with technology in the naive assumption that what is good for adults must also be good for children."*
> —*Gordon Neufeld, PhD, and Gabor Maté, MD, in* Hold On to Your Kids

best, as one mom of two teen girls discovered. "As a parent, I have always had a gut feeling about the negative consequences of teens and phones," she said. "Unfortunately, we started with all access. So for us, we are working our way backwards with our daughter's smartphone use. We have been bit by bit taking away her privileges. We are down to her phone being kept 100 percent out of her bedroom (day and night) and there is no more Snapchat! Hooray! Next up, we are transferring to text only."

It can be daunting to contemplate your teen's reaction if you even mention taking the smartphone away for a season. But be encouraged—plenty of families have done just that and have seen life-changing benefits.

Look at the situation like a coach managing a team. Good coaches formulate a plan, and they aren't afraid to take bold action when needed. Confident with their direction, they do what's best for their players and team. They know that any change may be met with pushback—moans and groans—from the team. So, as a good parent-coach, expect pushback, but don't be fazed by it.

Making this decision will require you to be really honest with your child. Start with a simple apology, saying something like this to your teen: "We have learned a lot about the brain science behind smartphone use and we made a mistake by allowing too much access too soon. Now we are making adjustments. We love you and we want you to spend more time together with your friends and with your family." Don't let it become a long, drawn-out argument.

Your goal is to win your child back into your family. This change is just for a season. Remind your teen that no is not forever; it's just no for now. If the smartphone has taken an unhealthy position in your child's life, the adjustment will be harder, but remember that taking a break is not the end of the world—even though your teen may react as if it is.

Think back to the list of problems my daughter never experienced in high school because she wasn't involved in social media drama. You may be sparing your child from "the end of the world"—the many tragic results we're seeing from cyberbullying, for example—when you reduce her smartphone and social media access. When you review the scientific information in Chapter 5, you'll see that by rethinking the smartphone decision, you may help your teen decrease the risk of a long list of mental health problems including anxiety, depression, and suicidal ideations.

"We need to stop thinking of smartphones as harmless," said Jean Twenge, a psychology professor at San Diego State University who studies generational trends, in an interview with the Associated Press. "There's a tendency to say, 'Oh, teens are just communicating with their friends.'

Monitoring kids' use of smartphones and social media is important, and so is setting reasonable limits." [23]

Taking a Step Back

As you contemplate how to reduce smartphone use, you may find it helpful to get a basic phone to replace the smartphone. The other option is to have a family basic phone that stays charged in the kitchen until the teen heads

out for an event or job such as babysitting, when she actually needs to use the phone as the tool it was meant to be.

Tips for Setting Responsible Limits:
- **Create a family social media account.** Keep this account, "The Smith Family Instagram," for example, on your phone or home computer instead of allowing each teen to have his own private account. He can still follow a few interests and friends on the family account. Again, this allows the phone to become a tool, not an appendage. Teens do not need their own accounts despite what the culture and their friends say. And they definitely should not have privacy on any social media. Accountability at every age is necessary for them to develop maturity.

- **Relocate apps from small screens to large screens.** Another option is to move all social media apps from her phone to her laptop or the family computer. This will not eliminate the content temptations, but it is a first line of defense to cut back on the sheer amount of time spent on the phone. When social media is no longer in her pocket or purse, your teen will naturally use it much less.

- **Limit to 20 minutes a day.** Any time using a smartphone can still negatively affect your teen, but nine hours a day is over the top. Allowing teens to use their phones excessively does not help them or teach mature limit setting. Most teens can't set these limits, but a good parent-coach can be the guide they need.

Tips for Taking Back the Phone:
- **Prepare for change.** Finding another family who feels like it's time for a phone break will help both you and your teen. Partner with them and get educated together. Read through a book from the resources page on our website or watch some of our videos together, then discuss the physical and emotional effects of screen overuse. Agree on a plan and go for it. The benefits of adding some friends to your team are many. For one, you will be helping the teens in both families develop better friendships by spending more time together.

- **Replace and refill.** Replace your teen's smartphone with a basic phone and revisit some of his abandoned hobbies. This will initially take more effort on your part as he will need lots of encouragement and affirmation along the way. Keep this process positive and begin trying some new activities together. Set up social plans with their friends every week till they can do it on their own.

- **Rebuild your family connection.** Phone overuse frequently leads to lost connections within the family. When your teens are more likely to turn to their phones (social media, texts, and even strangers) than their parents for life guidance, peer orientation has supplanted the parent connection, and it's time to win them back into your family. This is best accomplished through one-on-one time with your teen and time together as a family. Taking a weekend away with no agenda except to get to know your kids again is a great place to start. Connections are not hard to build, but they do take some time and patience.

9 Don't Just Survive: Thrive!

If you have not started the smartphone experiment in your home yet, let me encourage you to delay it. Start with a basic phone through high school and don't doubt your decision; your kids will learn how to use technology just fine. They will be more prepared for the real world without their smartphone.

If your teen already has a smartphone and you feel like she can resist the temptations and distractions, that's great! But if you sense that the phone is not making your teen a better person, and you are leaning toward replacing or radically reducing her smartphone use, let me encourage you to do just that. I have never met a parent of young adults who has said, "I wish I had given my teen a smartphone earlier than I did."

How do you know when your teen is ready for a smartphone? She is ready when she is mature, emotionally stable, well-connected to your family, and proficient in a variety of life skills. He is ready when his family ties are stronger than his ties to his peers. The timing of this decision depends not on a formula or a universal age, but rather on a parent's careful assessment and intuition. Only you know when she can stand on her own two feet without the crutch of a smartphone. When teens are not craving social media, then they are actually ready for it.

Be bold and be happy during these fleeting years when your teens need your direction the most. Don't let a device replace your leadership role in their lives. Plan special one-on-one times with each child to reinforce your relationships. Have a group of their friends over this weekend for some non-tech fun like making pizza and playing a fun board game together. Will they think that is corny? Sure they will, but they will love it! Just smile a lot, dust off your sense of humor and do it anyway.

Is it really possible for a teen to grow up today without a smartphone? You bet it is. I hope for you and your family that you can experience the same blessings that we have found by taking this less-traveled path. After all, close connections and togetherness with the people we love is what we all crave, even more than a smartphone.

Some Advice From Families Just Like Yours

"If I had to do it all over again, I would not give my kids a smartphone till the end of high school. It is my biggest regret as a parent."

—Mom of three children

"None of my daughters got iPhones till ninth grade; we thought they were mature enough. Boy were we wrong: fake Instagram and Snapchat accounts (after we said no to both of those platforms); horrible texting to perfect strangers. If we had to do it all over again, we would have delayed the iPhone for as long as possible. That one bad decision really damaged our relationships with our girls."

—Parents of two daughters

"My teen's smartphone was not making her a better person; we took it away."
—*Mom of two teen daughters*

"Taking away a smartphone is much harder than just not giving one at all."
—*Dad of three teens*

"All three of my teenagers have iPhones, which we regret giving to them, but seemed justifiable at the time. If I had to do it over again, my wife and I would have delayed it altogether. What a big waste of time and family relationships."
—*Dad of three older teens*

"Because we regret giving our three older children smartphones in their teen years, we decided to try a different approach with our youngest child, thanks to your advice. At 14, she got a basic phone with only talk-and-text features,

which was not easy to find! Nearly two years later, she is not 'attached to it.' She stays in touch with friends and can be part of their group texts, but she's not glued to the screen as so many of her peers are. We're grateful for the research Families Managing Media has done and all the information you've shared with us."

—Mom of four children

"I took my son's phone away for a month due to poor choices he had made. After the month was over, he asked me to keep it for another month! He was really enjoying his stress-free month, but was embarrassed to tell his friends that he didn't want his phone."

—Mom of one teen boy

"Giving our two daughters (now in high school) a smartphone was the worst parenting decision we have ever made. One of my daughters is seeing a counselor for social media anxiety. My youngest will not get a smartphone till college. Please continue your effort to educate other parents on this message; you will save so much heartache and worse."

—Mom of two daughters

How To Build ScreenStrong Kids in the Digital Age

Lead with a Coach's Heart
- Remember that parents, not kids, are in charge of all screens.
- Equip your child through conversations, not by allowing experimentation on a screen.
- Give a basic phone before a smartphone.

Build Life Skills and Independence First
- Teach life skills before handing over digital devices.
- Develop grit through extracurricular activities and hard work.
- Choose non-screen entertainment options.

Prioritize Family Time over Screen Time
- Delay video games and social media.
- Ensure screen habits reflect family core values.
- Create mindful connection times with family.

screen STRONG *Challenge*

ScreenStrong provides real solutions to prevent and reverse childhood screen addictions. Using medical science as our guide, we provide a fresh approach that helps parents regain direction and confidence as they face one of today's most crucial parenting challenges: raising kids in a digital world.

Do you need a plan to reduce screen time, but don't know where to start? Our ScreenStrong Challenge is a week-long break from video games and smartphones. It's designed to give your kids an opportunity to experience the things they've missed out on since gaming and social media stole their free time. It's a chance to step back, recharge, and reconnect with each other as a family.

Visit www.ScreenStrong.com for more information

Endnotes

1 Jean M. Twenge, Gabrielle N. Martin, and W. Keith Campbell, (2018). "Decreases in Psychological Well-Being Among American Adolescents After 2012 and Links to Screen Time During the Rise of Smartphone Technology." *Emotion*. Advance online publication. http://dx.doi.org/10.1037/emo0000403.

2 Jenny Marie. "Millennials-and-Mental-Health." NAMI, www.nami.org/Blogs/NAMI-Blog/December-2017/Millennials-and-Mental-Health, (Dec. 1, 2017).

3 Sigal Sharf. "Mental Disorders Tied To Smartphones." *Anxiety.org*, www.anxiety.org/smartphones-may-increase-stress, (April 2, 2013).

4 Jean M. Twenge, Thomas E. Joiner, Megan L. Rogers, and Gabrielle N. Martin, "Increases in Depressive Symptoms, Suicide-Related Outcomes, and Suicide Rates Among U.S. Adolescents After 2010 and Links to Increased New Media Screen Time." htbp://journals.sagepub.com/doi/full/10.1177/2167702617723376, (Nov. 14, 2017).

5 Ashley Welch. "What's behind the Rise in Youth Suicides?" *CBS News*, CBS Interactive, www.cbsnews.com/news/suicide-youth-teens-whats-behind-rise/, (Nov. 21, 2017).

6 John Nicholls. "6 Reasons Your Teen's Life Is More Stressful than Your Own." *The Washington Post*, WP Company, https://www.washingtonpost.com/news/parenting/wp/2017/05/15/6-reasons-your-teens-life-is-more-stressful-than-your-own/, (May 15, 2017).

7 "The Mere Presence of Your Smartphone Reduces Brain Power, Study Shows." *UT News | The University of Texas at Austin*, https://news.utexas.edu/2017/06/26/the-mere-presence-of-your-smart-phone-reduces-brain-power, (July 11, 2017).

8   Gordon Neufeld and Maté Gabor. *Hold On to Your Kids: Why Parents Need To Matter More than Peers.* (A.A. Knopf Canada, 2004.)

9   Richard Freed, PhD. *Wired Child: Reclaiming Childhood in a Digital Age.* (North Charleston, SC: CreateSpace Independent Publishing, 2015.)

10 Trevor Haynes. "Dopamine, Smartphones & You: A battle for your time." Science in the News, Harvard University, The Graduate School of Arts and Sciences, http://sitn.hms.harvard.edu/flash/2018/dopamine-smartphones-battle-time/, (May 1, 2018).

11 Dr. Daniel J. Siegel, MD. *Brainstorm: The Power and Purpose of the Teenage Brain.* (New York: Jeremy P. Tarcher/Penguin, 2013.)

12 Frances E. Jensen, MD, and Amy Ellis Nutt. *The Teenage Brain: a Neuroscientist's Survival Guide to Raising Adolescents and Young Adults.* (New York: HarperCollins, 2015.)

13 "Addiction by the Numbers." National Center of Addiction and Substance Abuse. Center on Addiction, www.centeronaddiction.org, (Jan. 1, 2018).

14 Charles Duhigg. *The Power of Habit: Why We Do What We Do in Life and Business.* (New York: Random House, 2014.)

15 Stuart Wolpert. "In our digital world, are young people losing the ability to read emotions?" UCLA Newsroom, http://newsroom.ucla.edu/releases/in-our-digital-world-are-young-people-losing-the-ability-to-read-emotions, (Aug. 21, 2014).

16 Sherry Turkle. *Reclaiming Conversation: The Power of Talk in a Digital Age.* (New York: Penguin Books, 2016). Borba, M. (2017).

17 Michele Borba. *UnSelfie: Why Empathetic Kids Succeed in Our All-About-Me World.* (New York: Touchstone, 2017.)

18 "How Porn Affects The Brain," Fight the New Drug, https://fightthenewdrug.org/overview/, (June 30, 2018).

19 "Distracted Driving Raises Crash Risk," National Institutes of Health, NIH Research Matters, https://www.nhtsa.gov/risky-driving/distracted-driving, (Jan. 13, 2014).

20 Melanie Hempe. "7 Reasons Why Your Teen Smartphone Contract Will Not Work." Families Managing Media, http://www.familiesmanagingmedia.com/7-reasons-why-your-teen-smartphone-contract-will-not-work/, (2016).

21 Chris Weller. "Silicon Valley parents are raising their kids tech-free — and it should be a red flag." Business Insider, http://www.businessinsider.com/silicon-valley-parents-raising-their-kids-tech-free-red-flag-2018-2, (Feb.18, 2018).

22 Margo Gardner, Jodie Roth, and Jeanne Brooks-Gunn. "Adolescents' Participation in Organized Activities and Developmental Success 2 and 8 Years after High School: Do Sponsorship, Duration, and Intensity Matter? *Developmental Psychology*, American Psychological Association, http://psycnet.apa.org/doiLanding?doi=10.1037%2F0012-1649.44.3.814, (May 2008).

23 Lindsey Tanner. "Rise in teen suicide, social media coincide; is there link?" Associated Press, https://www.apnews.com/c8d46d63494d4871b2bbdfc45efc459e, (Nov. 14, 2017).

About the Author

Melanie Hempe is the Founder and President of Families Managing Media, a national nonprofit organization that offers a countercultural approach to eliminating childhood screen dependency. Through its flagship ScreenStrong initiative and the 7-day ScreenStrong Challenge, FMM empowers parents to pause or delay the most addictive types of screen use by their kids, while emphasizing the importance of developing life skills.

Through her many speaking engagements at local workshops and conferences around the country, Melanie brings together her compelling personal story and her command of the emerging research on childhood screen addiction to provide practical solutions to struggling families. Her work has been featured in local and national media including *Psychology Today, Thrive-Global, The Wall Street Journal, NPR,* and *CBS.*

Melanie holds a Bachelor of Science in Nursing from Emory University and is the author of three books. She lives in North Carolina with her husband and their four children.

Made in the USA
Columbia, SC
27 March 2022